Most women I meet genuinely want to declutter but don't know where to start. Those that embark on the process often fail because of lack of knowledge or the incorrect mindset. Understandably, some women don't feel comfortable opening their private space to another or may be unable to justify the cost of hiring a professional. Others simply better enjoy the process alone.

Every woman I've ever met has had some form of struggle with her wardrobe and, without fail, everyone who declutters feels more in control, confident, and stylish.

Declutter Therapy™ the ultimate wardrobe decluttering experience empowers you to declutter your personal space. This expert guide equips you with the knowledge, tools, and confidence for life-long decluttering and shopping.

As I was creating Declutter Therapy™, several people asked me if it would focus solely on the wardrobe or the entire house. To me, the wardrobe is possibly the most significant space in a woman's home. We interact with it first thing in the morning and last thing at night and it stores so much - physically, mentally, and emotionally. Decluttering is contagious. Getting your wardrobe in order first and foremost will motivate and inspire you to take on the rest of your home.

I've always loved writing and have written and edited extensively for years. Declutter Therapy™ has allowed me to combine my very favourite interests – writing, style, decluttering, organising, charity, and the environment. I hope you enjoy the process as much as I've loved putting this guide together.

Happy Decluttering,
Breda Stack

testimonials

I felt like I was in a fashion cave for about a year, pregnant and post-baby. Now that I am slowly getting my body back I have been really craving some style in my life. In many ways Declutter Therapy™ has allowed me to begin again "stylistically". It really was a great opportunity to figure out who I am, with a baby and without. It has allowed me to free up some well-needed space in my wardrobe by learning to let go of many of my unwanted clothes, some of which were sentimental and valuable. It was with much satisfaction I was able to give my unloved items to family, friends and the local charity. I am really enjoying my clutter-free wardrobe and now the only clothes that belong there are clothes I wear that make me look and feel great. **Karen**

Declutter Therapy™ is so different to anything I've seen and is what women everywhere have been crying out for! I just loved the thought-provoking content and the beautiful presentation. It was like an indulgent diary with all the interactive little exercises! The process was insightful and thorough but still gentle and has made me feel much more relaxed and comfortable with change. A must-have experience! **Angela**

I spent years saying I'd get someone in to help me declutter but I never did – I'm a private person and it was just too embarrassing to let anyone into my wardrobe. Not alone did I finally declutter with Declutter Therapy™ but we also cleared out the spare room and donated five big bags to charity! It was such a relief to be free from all that stuff. I find myself thinking about the Selective Shopping guidelines when I go shopping. Things I would have settled for before just don't seem good enough for my wardrobe now and instead of buying items for the sake of it, I come home with clothes that I actually look forward to wearing. I can't tell you how exciting that is! **Laura**

ULTIMATE WARDROBE DECLUTTERING EXPERIENCE

Breda Stack

v1.0

Published in Ireland in 2012
ISBN 978-0-9573421-0-1

Design by Little Blue Studio *www.littlebluestudio.ie*
DVD by BMB Films *www.bmbfilms.com*
Printed by City Print *www.cityprint.ie*
Published by LifeStyle Coach *www.lifestylecoach.ie*

Acknowledgements

I'd like to thank the many people who have enthusiastically supported Declutter Therapy™ from the outset, not least my very patient husband Ronan! A special mention to Moira Geary for inspiring me to do what I love, Gaye Moore for her sound advice, Bryan O' Brien for his brilliant videography and Elaine Hennessey for her exemplary design skills and commitment to this project. Finally, I'd like to express gratitude to Dorothy Fitzgerald, Nora Collins, Tracy Aspel and Bobby Ramos for their sharp and constructive review comments and to Marion and Paddy Stack for their invaluable help throughout the process.

to my family

Introduction

Welcome to Declutter Therapy™ the ultimate wardrobe decluttering experience.

My story

As a child and young teenager I spent much of my time arranging my dolls, clothes, and fancy paper collection. I've always felt happier, more creative, and grounded when my physical environment is in order, be it a tidy kitchen, clean car or an efficient desktop. Strangely, being organised gives me both a sense of control and freedom. I guess my true calling was evident from an early age!

Over the years I've explored number of areas including Media and Communications, Interior Design, Life Coaching, and Style Consultancy, always with a view to developing a unique and meaningful business concept. I committed ten years to Information Technology before leaving to focus on LifeStyle Coach, my styling and wardrobe decluttering company. Understanding the complex link between style and confidence on a personal level was a major driving force behind the business.

Apart from throwing out the odd worn or outdated item, I'd never felt the need to declutter until I was in my late twenties. Dealing with weight gain for the first time in my life, I suddenly reached a point where 90% of my wardrobe no longer fitted me or represented my age, lifestyle or personal taste. I stopped enjoying style and, as dramatic as it sounds, I definitely went through an identity crisis.

To help me confront my problems I started to declutter my wardrobe. At first it was slow and painful, but it got easier and more fulfilling with each session. As my self-awareness increased I became more focused and confident - not just in my style but in other areas of my life. Decluttering helped me to accept change, regain control, and redefine who I wanted to be. It was the therapy needed to put my life back on track. Needless to say, I've been a true convert ever since!

Creating Declutter Therapy™

Over the past few years, I've worked with hundreds of women in the area of Wardrobe Decluttering with exciting and inspiring results. Privileged to gain deep insights into the colourful and intimate relationships between women and their wardrobes, I've seen many interesting patterns emerge.

Declutter therapy™

ULTIMATE WARDROBE DECLUTTERING EXPERIENCE

Declutter Therapy™ Instructions

Declutter Therapy™ the ultimate wardrobe decluttering experience is designed to ensure that the wardrobe decluttering process is as efficient, enjoyable, and therapeutic for you as possible. This guide has everything you need to declutter successfully. It contains information, steps, guidelines, and tips as well as interactive checklists and exercises. Simply follow the process, part by part and page by page.

Within this book you'll find your Declutter Therapy™ DVD which includes the following:

- Chapter 1: Introduction (00:33)
- Chapter 2: 8 Commonly-Heard Decluttering Excuses (03:38)
- Chapter 3: Repurposing Objects for Storage (01:44)
- Chapter 4: Wardrobe Organisation (01:31)
- Chapter 5: 10 TOP TIPS for Decluttering (03:08)
- Chapter 6: Wardrobe Decluttering Visualisation Exercise (03:41)

You can enjoy this DVD any time but to really get the most out of it, watch it in full after you've read Declutter Therapy™ Part 5: Organisation and Storage.

The DVD runtime is 14:46.

Part 1

MINDSET

Declutter Therapy™

Declutter Therapy™ Mindset

Our physical environment has a direct effect on how we feel, regardless of whether we're consciously aware of this fact. Just about every tangible object around us evokes positive or negative emotions and associations.

The more items we own the more financial, physical, mental, and emotional energy they demand, so the less control we have over our daily lives. Everything in this world has a natural lifecycle and when we become too dependent on material possessions we lose sight of what life is really about.

As with all positive life-changing exercises, the key to long-term success is a change in mindset. The Declutter Therapy™ Mindset promotes a conscious shift around the value and meaning of material possessions so you can enjoy a happier, more fulfilled life.

The Declutter Therapy™ Mindset reflects the ancient Chinese system of Feng Shui by encouraging positive energy, movement, air, light, space, cleanliness, and balance in our physical environment. This mix of art and science shows how placing an object with intent and purpose helps you to change the belief and emotion around the object. Feng Shui theories are aligned with a modern understanding that all aspects of our lives are interlinked, and a change in any particular area has a knock-on effect on other areas.

When we take control of our living space we begin to think and feel differently. Decluttering helps us to gain perspective and establishes a balance between respecting material goods and being dominated by them. It's just like taking a snapshot of your life and putting it under a microscope for analysis – it is effectively an exercise in clearing out the mind.

Decluttering makes a big, brave statement. You are saying:

- I accept my current requirements
- I am becoming aware of the link between object and emotion
- I am reevaluating my priorities

Despite how inherently disorganised we believe we are, it takes just three to six weeks to develop the Declutter Therapy™ Mindset. This new pattern of thinking opens us up to a healthier relationship with our physical environment. Expect to go through a range of positive and negative feelings and emotions as you learn to see things differently. Take refuge in the fact that everything you experience is valuable and serves its purpose in helping you to understand, change, and move forward.

Declutter Therapy™ Feelings and Emotions

Circle those that stand out for you, or add your own.

Amazed Authentic Ashamed Balanced
Brave Calm Cheerful Clear Conflicted
Doubtful Empowered Energised
Excited Exposed Expressive
Fantastic Fearful Free Frustrated
Fun-loving Guilty Happy Hesitant
Impatient Impulsive Inspired Irritated
Joyous Keen Knowing Liberated
Light Motivated Nostalgic Open
Overwhelmed Panicked Passionate
Peaceful Pleased Powerful Practical
Pressurised Purposeful Real Regretful
Relieved Sad Satisfied Scared
Sentimental Spirited Stressed Tired
Trusting Understanding Unsure
Vigorous Vulnerable Zealous

____

____

____

____

____

Clutter Defined

Individual lifestyles and personalities require a different balance of material possessions, and so how we classify clutter inevitably varies. Broadly speaking, clutter is any physical item which you don't love, want, need or use. In today's fast-paced society, our tastes and needs continually evolve and much of what we own becomes outdated, worn out or superfluous.

Material clutter becomes mental jumble and emotional baggage, weighing us down so we feel flat and overwhelmed. Clutter distracts from the positives in life and creates a barrier to living in the present. In simple terms, clutter is anything that doesn't make you feel good.

How Possessions Become Clutter

To get the better of clutter, it's important to understand how it accumulates. Our beliefs and values play a primary role in how we relate to our physical surroundings. Over time, we've learned and adopted thinking and behaviour from ancestors in the quest for survival. Historically, some cultures and ethnicities have suffered great shortages and stashing, sparing, and saving have become the norm.

Over the last few decades we've enjoyed more expendable income than ever before, so consequentially we're shopping more. The addictive, natural high we get from shopping gives us an instant lift, helping us to forget our problems and stresses. Clever marketing strategies bombard us with messages for sales, designer products, and luxury brands, appealing to our vulnerabilities. We're constantly told that physical possessions will give our lives more meaning and make us feel more important and attractive. Trends change quickly and there's also a recent draw towards cheaper 'disposable fashion', which, ironically, we're not giving away.

The thrifty mindset inherited from parents, grandparents, and institutions is very much in conflict with today's impulsive, consumer-driven society. We have too much, but yet we struggle with giving anything away. Practically speaking, we have limited storage space, so there's only so much we can gather before our homes begin to burst at the seams.

Clutter tends to attract clutter, and it can grow slowly and stealthily. Deep-rooted attachments to possessions can be very destructive. In extreme cases, a build up of clutter can develop into hoarding, often symptomatic of mental or emotional dysfunction.

Obstacles to Decluttering

There are many obstacles to decluttering – some we can identify and others are safely tucked away in our subconscious, out of awareness. Although the need to declutter nags at our conscience, we often become paralysed by over-analysis. We adopt many beliefs to help justify the problems around us such as lack of time or organisational skills, but they rarely reflect the reality.

As with many things in life, fear is a fundamental block to decluttering. This fear can present itself in different ways, but it is all connected to a resistance to change. Whether the fear seems rational or not doesn't matter. Understanding what's been holding you back is empowering in your quest to take action.

Use the following checklist to help you gain clarity around your decluttering fears. It's ok if you're not quite sure what's stopping you - you can revisit this at any time.

My Fears

- ☐ Opening up to the unknown
- ☐ Throwing out items by accident
- ☐ Having less
- ☐ Losing a sense of security or self-worth
- ☐ Relinquishing control of routine or environment
- ☐ Being overwhelmed by the work-load
- ☐ Facing reality
- ☐ Lack of time or energy
- ☐ Uncovering 'skeletons in the closet'
- ☐ Destroying sentimental memories and attachments
- ☐ Experiencing shame, guilt or embarrassment
- ☐ Limited knowledge around the functional or financial value of items
- ☐ Lack of support
- ☐ Disconnecting with the past
- ☐ Defying norms and attitudes enforced in the past
- ☐ Letting go
- ☐ Inability to keep things tidy and organised
- ☐ Lack of understanding of the process
- ☐ Worrying about what others will think or say
- ☐ Limited appreciation of the benefits of decluttering

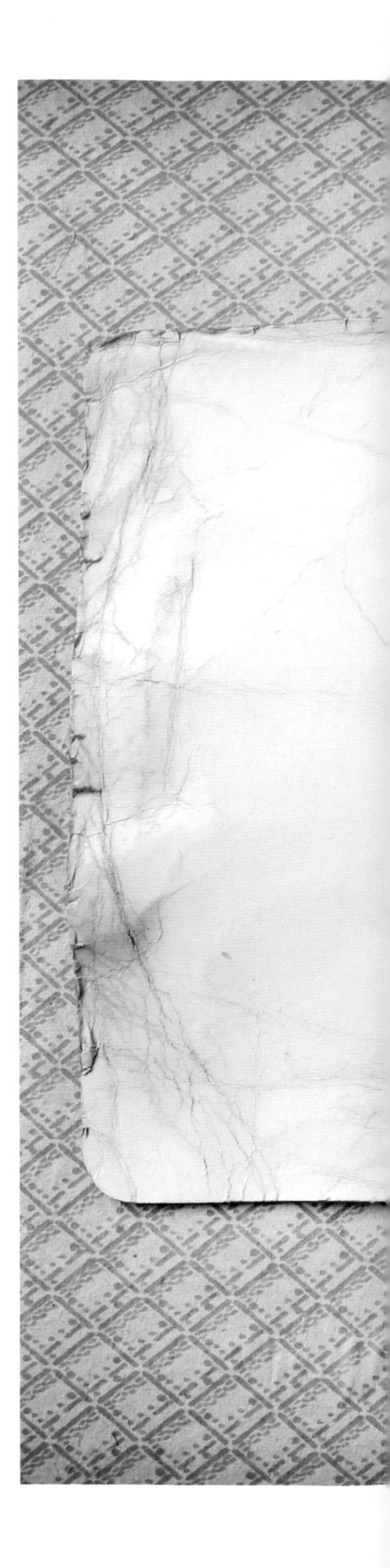

Time to Declutter

There are many practical reasons you may want to declutter including insufficient space, inadequate storage solutions, poor organisation, too many items or items which are no longer inspiring, suitable or seasonal. Your store of possessions may be causing friction with a partner or family member, and you might like to restore harmony.

Acknowledging the struggle with your physical possessions is the first step to change. In official terms, decluttering can take the guise of a gentle Spring Clean, a routine wardrobe clear out or a life-transforming exercise. Regardless of the approach, it offers emotional release and the potential for radical transformation.

Symbolic milestones and major life-events such as deaths, divorces, babies, house moves, and career transitions invariably lead to a change in lifestyle. Such dramatic episodes bring new physical requirements, while also having a profound effect on our thinking and behaviour. Unsurprisingly, these experiences often lead to major decluttering sessions.

In recessionary times we also tend to question our relationship with material goods – many of us become disillusioned with extravagance and aspire to a more holistic existence. As we get older we're attracted to a simpler way of living, and the space decluttering creates symbolises freedom and openness.

Decluttering your wardrobe

Personal style and self-image are inextricably linked and this is nowhere more evident than the wardrobe, effectively a mirror to our lives. Our age, body, lifestyle, and personal style are all in a constant state of change, and when we resist or ignore the inevitable our wardrobe holds the evidence.

The wardrobe is most often located in the bedroom, the space where we retreat to relax and sleep. This emotional nucleus is typically where we store secrets, hopes, fears, and dreams, as well as joyous and painful reminders of the past.

Every morning we're greeted with garments that we've never worn and things that remind us of when we were younger, thinner or the day we fell out with our best friend. It's no surprise that we feel drained of energy before our day even begins.

As with anything you undertake, what you give out you'll get back in abundance. Deep-seated feelings and emotions make the wardrobe a difficult but yet extremely effective place to start decluttering.

Taking the time to evaluate your wardrobe and determine what has earned its place there makes it much easier to master your individual style.

your mission

You deserve to wake up every morning to a wardrobe where each item fits and flatters you, reflects your lifestyle, age, and personality, and - most importantly - makes you feel good.

To help keep you in the Declutter Therapy™ Mindset, consider what successful completion of the process means to you. Draw a picture, attach an image or write some words below – even add a 'before' and 'after' photo of your wardrobe to help inspire your efforts.

My Declutter Therapy™ Success

Part 2

Benefits

Declutter Therapy™ Benefits

The process of decluttering offers many practical and holistic benefits which can be experienced immediately. By continuing to embrace the Declutter Therapy™ Mindset you'll carry on reaping the therapeutic rewards.

Practical Benefits

- Creates a more effective and versatile wardrobe
- Ensures items suit your body shape and colouring
- Enables a style which is age, climate, and lifestyle-appropriate
- Allows you to develop your individual style
- Creates a tidy and organised system
- Enables a fresher, cleaner living environment
- Increases visibility and accessibility of items
- Frees up and maximises storage space
- Allows you to uncover missing or hidden items
- Helps you to identify and overcome negative shopping patterns
- Encourages you to become more budget-focused
- Enables you to make money from your possessions
- Allows others to benefit from your unwanted items

Holistic Benefits

- Increases time and energy
- Improves focus, motivation, and confidence
- Creates a sense of freedom
- Releases pent-up stress, anger, and frustration
- Increases a sense of identity and self-worth
- Encourages creativity
- Enables self-awareness and self-discovery
- Helps you to take control of your living space
- Celebrates variety and selectivity
- Helps you to assess and reorder priorities
- Decreases dependency on physical possessions
- Enhances gratitude and respect for what you have
- Allows you to process and accept the past
- Helps to cut ties with negative feelings and associations
- Enables you to enjoy the present
- Embraces change, growth, and excitement
- Opens you up to potential and opportunity

The Mini-Decluttering Task

It's only natural that you may feel a sense of dread, worry or self-doubt in relation to the work that lies ahead. To help you to develop confidence in both yourself and the Declutter Therapy™ process, carry out the following mini-decluttering task.

Think of one item you own that you know you will never wear again. Write it down.

____

Without deliberating, walk to your wardrobe. Remove the item, put it into a plastic bag and immediately place it out of sight in a less-frequented area of your home.

Acknowledge how it feels to have taken the vital first step to a decluttered wardrobe and be pleased with your efforts!

Part 3

Distributing unwanted items

Distributing unwanted items

Although you haven't commenced decluttering just yet, now is a good time to think about how you might dispose of your unwanted items. These are anything you're not keeping, binning or sending to be cleaned, repaired or altered.

Choosing how to distribute your goods in advance will help to keep you focused as you declutter. Knowing exactly who'll benefit from your items will incentivise you to be braver during your decision-making, and you'll be more likely to move items on sooner.

Anything you bin ends up in landfill sites but this can needlessly shorten the life of unwanted items. There are a number of great ways to extend the lifespan of goods so they keep giving value. You may even decide to distribute them between a number of places depending on their financial worth, condition, and sentimental value.

It's best to dispose of your unwanted items in the manner you originally intended as soon as you've decluttered. Crucially, many people fail at this point as the bags become a permanent fixture in the spare room, hall, garage, attic or car, and the problem remains. As long as the bags inhabit another area of your home you'll risk the temptation to rummage through and second-guess yourself. Trust your initial gut feeling and don't undo all your hard work. Quickly and confidently distributing your items immediately after decluttering can determine the success of the whole process.

Give

It's very rewarding to pass on the proceeds of your decluttering to appreciative family and friends. One man's trash is indeed another man's treasure and it's great to see others enjoying something we no longer need. Giving is especially fulfilling when your mother has been unashamedly eyeing up your once-loved red shoes or your friend would be grateful for the suit you no longer need.

Think twice before offering your unwanted items to just anyone. Some people find it impossible to refuse a brimming bag and in this case it's likely that your clutter will just become theirs. Consider the age, taste, size, and lifestyle of the would-be recipients before you offer your goods. It's always easier to pass on items like scarves, jewellery, and handbags where the size and cut aren't as relevant to the wearer. Invite friends and family to your home as soon as you've decluttered and let them take what they genuinely want. Keeping items under your own roof ensures you can distribute the things your loved ones don't snap up quickly and effectively.

Sell

The idea of making money from unwanted possessions is very appealing and little-worn, dressier items in perfect condition always attract attention. However, unless your items are rare, expensive or highly desirable it can be difficult to make much money. Selling your items can be time-consuming and inconvenient and many online auction websites are flooded with once desirable dresses and occasion-wear. Be aware also that if you are selling from home and having little success you're more likely to reinstate an item back in your wardrobe.

Trends change quickly, as do consumer demands. Most items of clothing, footwear, and accessories lose the bulk of their value after just a year and high-street clothing loses its value particularly quickly. You've a better chance of making money if you're selling vintage - roughly classed as anything more than 25 years old - in the form of dresses, coats, handbags or jewellery. The bespoke design and durability typically associated with vintage appeals to collectors, helping to retain its value.

Options for selling your unwanted items are:

- live auctions
- online auction and shopping websites
- print and online advertisements
- car boot/garage/yard sales
- second-hand shops
- vintage shops
- pay-per-weight clothing outlets

Exchange

Exchanging unwanted items is always a popular option, especially as no money changes hands. With so many overloaded wardrobes it appeals to lovers of the environment as well as fans of vintage and high-quality, designer goods. The focus is on giving and receiving and there's often a link with charitable causes. Ways to exchange your unwanted items include:

- style swap events
- swap shops

Donate

Donating to charity engenders a sense of social contribution and your unwanted items will be greatly appreciated by those who receive. This feel-good exercise reminds us of how fortunate we are and it's important to know that your once-loved possessions will help others. Donating soothes the conscience and helps lessen feelings of guilt around expensive or unworn items. It creates a new lifecycle for unwanted goods as an item is sold for a fair price to someone who values it. Generated funds are then utilised by the charity to benefit their cause.

Donating is a very straightforward method of distributing your unwanted items and some charities will conveniently call to your home to pick up goods. Enquire about collection dates and ensure your bags are not gathering dust in the hall. If there's a real fear of you sifting through your items again, it's best to make that journey to the shop yourself. Beware of unscrupulous illegal charities that collect clothing from outside your door - always check the registered charity number before you donate.

Generally speaking, charities accept most types of good-condition clothing, footwear, accessories, and jewellery with the likely exception of swimwear, underwear, and nightwear. At times, charities request particular items or enforce temporary restrictions on the goods they'll take in. The fact that there are so many worthy local, national, and international causes to support makes it easy to find a charity that resonates with you.

You can donate your unwanted items to:

- charity shops
- charity events
- charity clothes bins
- community groups, shelters, schools, hospitals, etc.

Recycle

There are a number of good reasons to recycle your unwanted clothing and footwear. Products made with synthetic or man-made fibres don't decompose and so exert pressure on landfills. Wool, although a natural fibre, produces methane when decomposing which adds to greenhouse gas emissions. The recycling process doesn't require harsh chemicals and it reduces the need for natural resources in the production of new clothing and transportation to the shop shelf.

Some charities - especially those supporting Third World causes - benefit from modern recycling programmes.

Textile recycling can be inexpensive and convenient for materials which are suited to the process. Clean, dry clothing and pairs of footwear in good condition are generally accepted, but check local guidelines and policies in advance before handing anything in.

Ways to dispose of your unwanted goods through recycling include:

- textile recycling plants
- recycling events for charities, community centres, schools, etc.

Textile recycling is a socially-responsible and environmentally-friendly method of discarding your unwanted items. It's suitable for objects which are in good condition but may be difficult to give, sell, exchange or donate.

part 4

selective shopping

Declutter Therapy™

selective shopping

Decluttering is the perfect incentive to become more thoughtful and discerning in the clothing, footwear, accessories, and jewellery you buy. It's an opportunity to acknowledge and learn from any previous style mistakes and understand what works for you.

The awareness the Declutter Therapy™ Mindset brings makes it difficult to revert to old shopping habits. It takes us beyond the point where we need an excessive number of material things to make us feel good or where we simply buy for the sake of it. Once we've decluttered we will always shop more strategically – we naturally want to protect ourselves from any regret, disappointment or guilt in getting rid of items in the future.

Selective shopping is empowering and liberating and applying your personal style filters gives you a real sense of strength. This more deliberate way of shopping isn't designed to instil deprivation and lack of excitement, nor should it dampen the thrill of the odd impulse buy. Discovering who you are and truly reflecting this in your style is satisfying and priceless.

The Five Elements of Selective Shopping

1. Experience
2. Budget
3. Requirements
4. Individuality
5. Desirability

Experience

Shopping is as much about experience as the items you buy and clothes shopping should always be positive. Again, it's all about mindset. Expect to enjoy your shopping trip. Don't put yourself under any pressure, even if you really need something specific. Tell yourself you're going for a light-hearted browse and if you start to feel overwhelmed or frustrated, go for a cup of coffee. Be careful who you take with you – not everyone's advice is worth taking! You want someone who will be enthusiastic and honest, but kind. Avoid anyone who tries to push their style ideals on you. For a fresh and professional viewpoint, avail of the free in-house personal shoppers provided by some retailers or hire a reputable Style Consultant.

The Shop

Being a more discerning shopper includes becoming more selective in where you spend your money. Whether it's rummaging for vintage treasures on dusty rails or modern, spacious aisles with items in every size, we all have a preference. If past experiences of a particular brand make you feel flat and uninspired before you even enter the store, simply avoid it. The marketing, advertising, PR, returns policies, staff, layout, smell, and music all help to create the right atmosphere - not to mind the effect the changing room mirrors and lighting have on us. Negative associations with a retailer can sometimes turn us off a perfectly acceptable item, so ask yourself how you really feel about a shop before you purchase. It's good to be open-minded, however. We often dismiss stores based on lack of knowledge, hearsay or the shop window but it's nice to get a different perspective when we finally venture in.

Be patient and take as much time as you need to make a decision before buying. If you return to the shop and the item is gone just trust that it wasn't meant to be! Try everything on. Misjudgements can be easily prevented by a brief session in the changing room.

If you've a strong social conscience and are passionate about ethical consumerism, investigate retailers' fair trade, environmental, and animal-friendly policies before you shop.

Shopping online

Buying online has become very popular and is particularly attractive for women who don't enjoy the shopping experience. Of course it's a gamble in terms of quality, cut, and sizing so for clothing and footwear it's best to stick to more recognised brands. It's especially a shot in the dark if you like to feel a fabric before you buy. Even though items bought online are a lot less likely to be worn, they're often not returned. Modern technology makes shopping for something specific or unique more feasible than ever but with no cash physically changing hands, it's easy to imagine how internet shopping can spiral out of control.

Budget

The Declutter Therapy™ Mindset advocates buying only items which enhance your life. This selective shopping is sympathetic to more limited finances, helping you to control spending and stick to a budget. You're much less likely to indulge in negative shopping patterns such as impulse buying or the repeat buying of a particular item or colour when you shop deliberately. You'll also be more mindful of keeping receipts and making prompt returns if necessary.

Many retailers now offer full or partial sales year-round. Sales are great, as long as you're on a mission. If you tend to get carried away at the sight of a red tag ask yourself if you'd pay full price for the item. To make an impression on a limited budget, classic items in neutral colours always look more luxurious. Be aware that cheaper brands generally offer less-generous sizing, harder-to-wear cuts, and flimsier fabrics. For quality clothing at competitive prices, cut-price designer outlets can be a great option.

Ensure any costly 'Investment Buy' lives up to its name by being timeless, versatile, and durable. If you need convincing, ask yourself if you'll still want to wear the item three years from now. Inexpensive accessories and jewellery keep your style seasonal and give a new lease of life to existing items – a statement necklace or scarf will really lift an old black shift dress. You could also relegate your less-worn dressier clothes to everyday-wear by adding casual elements – team a formal coat with jeans or a wrap dress with flat boots.

Tips for shopping on a budget

- Assess your wardrobe in advance
- Write a shopping list and stick to it
- Leave your credit card at home
- Calculate cost-per-wear of an item
- Consider expense of any alterations
- Check if an item requires dry cleaning
- Ask for a reduction at the counter

Requirements

Our requirements when shopping for clothing, footwear, accessories, and jewellery differ greatly, and relevant factors include age, body shape and size, and lifestyle activities.

Age

As most retailers target a younger, trend-conscious market, selective shopping becomes more difficult with age. Shopping from the mid-thirties onwards can be particularly challenging as the figure and personal taste mature significantly. Many women feel torn between the younger, high-street shops and the more traditionally-conservative boutique.

Body

Despite international attempts to standardise sizing in female clothing, it varies remarkably from one retailer to another, and even within the same retailer. Regardless of the size on the tag, every item you buy should fit you perfectly so it can be taken home and immediately enjoyed. Resist the urge to buy a smaller size to incentivise weight loss - this rarely works! It's hard enough to look at an item that reminds you of unsuccessful weight-loss attempts, not to mind the hard-earned money you've needlessly wasted.

Knowing your body shape is fundamental to successful shopping. You need to buy to accommodate your widest part, but this can be tricky if you're a different size on top and bottom. Many shops have cuts which tend to favour certain body shapes so learn which ones work best for you. Every item you buy should feel good on - avoid anything that pinches, itches or scratches. Contrary to popular belief, style and comfort aren't mutually exclusive. Shop around until you find something that ticks both boxes.

4
CONTRAST
55% LINEN
45% COTTON

Lifestyle

Selective shopping encourages you to test the relevance of everything you buy against your lifestyle. We tend to wear just about a third of our wardrobes, which means there are many items we rarely or never wear. We naturally buy fewer items for activities we enjoy less, like work or exercise, but rewearing the same few uninspiring items in an environment you don't love doesn't make things any better. Clothing, footwear, accessories, and jewellery for dressy occasions and fine weather are exciting and aesthetically appealing, but it's important to consider how an item will serve you. For a fully functional wardrobe, the contents should reflect the breakdown of your lifestyle activities.

Wardrobe versatility is key to a busy lifestyle, and we all want to buy clothes from which we'll get value. Shoes are a good example of items we buy a lot and seldom wear – many of us have dozens of pairs which lie forgotten in the depths of our wardrobes. Versatile wardrobe pieces are the basic foundations of an outfit. They're simple and classic but still look modern and current. You can pick up these wardrobe elements without any particular outfit in mind, and they can be dressed up or down. As they are plainer, they're less noticeable and are very adaptable, helping to increase the wearability of existing wardrobe items.

Create an effective and well-balanced wardrobe by buying mostly versatile items, allowing a little room for more colourful, patterned, and textured pieces. You'll always need more tops than bottoms too, as bottoms are generally darker, plainer, and more durable, and they tend to need less washing.

Versatile pieces incorporate:

- solid, block colours
- low-contrast patterns e.g. leopard print
- staple neutral shades e.g. cream, black, brown, grey
- pseudo-neutral shades e.g. navy or khaki
- dull metallic shades e.g. bronze or silver
- shoes and handbags in year-round fabrics e.g. plain matt leather

versatile 16-item capsule wardrobe for a woman of any age

(Left-to-right, top-to-bottom) lace top, trench coat, flat boots, plain watch, sunglasses, leopard print scarf, pearl necklace, court shoes, ballet flats, wrap dress, clutch, straight-leg jeans, large handbag, diamond stud earrings, blazer, plain white shirt

Capsule Wardrobe

A Capsule Wardrobe has between 6 and twenty-four items of clothing, footwear, accessories, and jewellery with complimentary themes and colours. It offers a number of complete and interchangeable outfits for a particular activity while reflecting body, age, and individual style requirements. The conscious selection of items within a capsule helps to streamline a wardrobe so you can quickly and effortlessly create a look.

The capsule system doesn't have to be restrictive - you can create as many budget, weather, and activity-appropriate capsules as you like. A good capsule epitomises versatility and can be worn for a number of activities. Keep your capsule fresh and interesting by introducing colour and pattern carefully and replacing items as they wear and date.

Individuality

Style is a great way to express yourself, and there's nothing more fulfilling than buying an item that defines your individual taste. Although the concepts of style and fashion are often confused, fashion often takes the individuality out of style.

Behind the rails of fashionable clothing lies a highly profitable industry that engages us with slick and expensive marketing campaigns. The fear of being 'out-of-fashion' lures us towards the latest collections so we feel more youthful and accepted. It's good to be choosy in the trends you adopt – give credit to your instinct and ignore much of what fashionistas say.

Shopping more selectively shouldn't prevent you from taking a style risk. Trying something new is exciting and helps to keep your wardrobe interesting – accessories and jewellery are again a fun and non-committal way of experimenting with different looks. Take comfort in the fact that it's impossible to go through life without making at least a few mistakes, and we learn so much from getting it wrong.

However clichéd it may seem, style is a journey. Keep your individual style relevant by letting it evolve with you.

L
o

Desirability

Finally, but essentially, you should truly love something before you buy it. It needs to inspire and thrill you, making you feel confident and attractive. You should be leaving the shop, bag in hand with a smiling face and singing heart or you should be tossing and turning all night with regret if you've left it behind. It's always better to come home empty-handed than with things you don't love.

Once you've made a purchase, try it on at home with the right elements and an open mind. Assess it objectively. It should conjure up the same positive emotions and feelings that it did in the shop.

Take control by extending the principles of selective shopping to everything you buy and your life will be simpler and happier.

Selective Shopping Guidelines

- Honour your budget
- Respect your requirements
- Reflect your individuality
- Follow your heart

travel

part 5

organisation and storage

Declutter Therapy™

organisation and storage

Ambience

The ambience of your living space is as important as convenience and practicality - remember that our physical environment influences us in many ways.

If you're not lucky enough to own a separate walk-in wardrobe, ensure you can truly switch off in the sanctuary of a tidy and organised bedroom. The view from your sleeping position at least should be attractive, calming, and clutter-free.

Tips for creating ambience in your bedroom

- Repaint/replace wardrobe doors
- Repaint/wallpaper inside of wardrobe
- Add spotlights to inside of wardrobe
- Change handles on drawers and doors
- Repaint bedroom walls
- Add lamps and mirrors for light and space

It's vital to have a full-length mirror in the space in which you put on your clothes. You're always less inclined to go to a mirror in another room to check an outfit, especially when you're stuck for time. Balancing in high heels on a bed or chair to gain access to a dresser mirror is never recommended!

organisation

We tend to use the middle of the wardrobe most so ensure the items that give you the biggest boost are those you see first. If you're trying to break the habit of wearing a lot of casual wear or sportswear, position it where you're less likely to choose it automatically. In terms of wardrobe ergonomics, place items within hand-reach if possible to help avoid unnecessary strain or accidents. For things that can't be accessed easily by hand, keep a strong step ladder or stool handy.

You're likely to forget about anything you can't see but if you can't make everything visible, clearly mark items with labels, stickers or photos. If wardrobe space is very restricted consider keeping coats, occasion-wear, and out-of-season items elsewhere.

There are a number of ways to organise your clothing and you should choose the one that works best for you. Decide on the optimum and most natural home for every item depending on fabric, size, and function.

You could group items as follows:

- visually (by colour, length, etc.)
- by activity
- by item

You can further categorise things to suit your requirements, e.g. first by item, then by colour.

Tips for increasing wardrobe efficiency

- ♡ Put a single item on each hanger
- ♡ Turn all clothes the right way out
- ♡ Position the tip of the hanger hook away from you on the rail
- ♡ Face the front of each hanging item in the same direction
- ♡ Button shirts and blouses so they don't fall off hangers
- ♡ Leave free space on the rail for easy movement

space

Remove as much as you can from the floor to create a flowing space that allows you to walk around unhindered. Make the most of existing wardrobe space by introducing or repositioning rails and shelves. Permanent or adjustable hanging rails work especially well if you have unused space at the top of your wardrobe.

Many older houses offer unusually-shaped room corners or attic roof space, greatly increasing storage potential. Redundant areas between architectural features and furniture can also be cleverly transformed into useful spots for shelves or boxes. Wall mounting a full-length mirror also helps save space, as do sliding wardrobe doors with mirrors. Wall space just under the ceiling is an area which is under-utilised in most houses and so is a practical storage option for out-of-season items.

Free-standing multi-level clothing rails with shelves are a good temporary solution and can work well in a spare room. For rails that don't come with a canvas or plastic cover, figure out a way to keep items protected.

Typically, limited wardrobe space is seen as a negative but one small wardrobe can be much more effective than a number of large, separate units.

Advantages of a small single wardrobe include:

- better head-to-toe outfit co-ordination
- more imaginative combination of colour, cut, and pattern
- less wardrobe space to fill
- less likely to make repeat buys

Storing unevenly-sized clothing, footwear, accessories, and jewellery always presents a challenge, and limited space is a life-long constraint. Your goal is to position items in as small an area as possible where they can still be seen and retrieved. The clever use of space allows you to create a natural home for everything. Aim to create a functional system that doesn't require detailed maps or indices.

Organisation Guidelines

- Minimal
- Visible
- Accessible
- Logical

solutions

Shopping for storage solutions is fun and there's an amazing selection of handy knick-knacks on the market to suit all requirements. It can be tempting to rush out and buy before you know what you need.

Adopt your Declutter Therapy™ Mindset and carefully consider how an object will benefit your living space. Some of the smartest storage solutions are very inexpensive and with a little imagination you can source very useful pieces, even repurposing items from around your own home.

A measuring tape is a vital tool in the selection of workable storage solutions. Measure and remeasure a space and record relevant details before you go shopping. Bring your measuring tape to the store so you can check the dimensions for yourself. Avoid objects that will cause obstruction or that will make valuable space redundant.

Storage solutions that are visible in your living area should be attractive and complimentary to the room decor and may even serve as a focal point.

clothing

Guard clothing from dust, dirt, damp, direct sunlight, and moths and other insects.

Good storage options include:

- drawer dividers
- shelf dividers
- heavy card/wooden/clear plastic boxes
- clear sealable/vacuum-packed plastic bags
- wicker baskets
- foldable/hanging laundry baskets
- hangers

Matching hangers create a sleek look and move efficiently on the rail. A sturdy, non-slip hanger in velvet, plastic or wood is preferable – use the correct type for suits, trousers, skirts, and jackets. Although thicker hangers take up more space on the rail, they allow clothes to sit well and are less likely to intertwine in the way wire hangers do.

Footwear

Footwear takes up a lot of space, and high heels and boots are especially hard to stow. Insufficient storage often results in damaged heels and the scuffing of delicate suede, satin or ornate shoes and sandals. If possible, keep season-appropriate footwear in the wardrobe together with clothes. Avoid wooden shoe racks where heels may get caught between planks.

Clever storage solutions include:

- shoe racks/wheels
- over-the-door shoe holders
- clear plastic shoe boxes
- clear plastic shoe bags
- cloth bags with drawstrings
- wooden boxes or wicker baskets placed on shelves
- clip hangers for boots

underwear

Although underwear typically falls under the clothing category, due to its size and delicate nature it is better to store it separately. Prevent damage to underwire bras and protect tights and other fine fabrics from snagging caused by zips, clasps and bra hooks.

Consider:

- small clear plastic boxes
- small clear sealable plastic bags
- small cloth bags with drawstrings
- drawer dividers

Accessories

Minimise damage to handbags and hats and protect flimsy items like silk scarves.

Workable solutions include:

- accessory rings
- wall boxes
- hat boxes
- small clear plastic boxes
- small clear sealable plastic bags
- small cloth bags with drawstrings
- small baskets
- drawer dividers and trays
- shelf dividers
- racks and hooks on walls or the back of doors

Jewellery

Rings, bracelets, brooches, earrings, necklaces, and watches are tricky to store. Prevent knotting, breaking, and tarnishing by choosing solutions which are not too deep and have lots of compartments.

Practical storage options for jewellery include:

- jewellery boxes and stands
- small clear plastic boxes
- small clear sealable plastic bags
- small cloth bags with drawstrings
- small drawer dividers and trays
- small racks and hooks on walls or the back of doors

storage solution Guidelines

- Hard-wearing
- Attractive
- Keeps items clean and protected
- Makes the most of existing space

Part 6

Toolkit and Preparation

DeclutterTherapy™

Toolkit and Preparation

Equip yourself with these useful items before you begin decluttering to help make your session more feasible.

Declutter Therapy™ Toolkit

- ☐ Full-length mirror
- ☐ Vacuum cleaner
- ☐ Polish and cloth
- ☐ Empty laundry container
- ☐ Large strong plastic bags
- ☐ Labels or stickers
- ☐ Markers
- ☐ Hangers
- ☐ Music system
- ☐ Room scent

Tips for managing your time and energy

- Set aside a full day to complete Preparation, Wardrobe Worthiness Test, and Tidy Up
- Keep 2 to 5 hours for Wardrobe Worthiness Test, depending on how many items you own
- Ensure you've no interruptions – put your phone on silent if necessary
- Take light breaks and plenty of food and water
- Work in natural light as much as you can

Declutter Therapy™ Preparation

1. Complete the Visualisation Exercise on your Declutter Therapy™ DVD
2. Play your favourite music in the background
3. Open curtains, blinds, windows, and doors if possible
4. Spray a natural air freshener, burn an essential oil or light a scented candle in a safe place
5. Clear floor space – temporarily move large items if you can
6. Make sure your bed is tidy and clear of any items
7. Create a clearly-marked system to allow for the different piles of clothing, e.g.:
    - return to wardrobe
    - laundry
    - dry cleaner
    - dressmaker/cobbler
    - give/sell/exchange/donate/recycle
    - bin
8. Gather up all clothing, footwear, accessories, and jewellery from your wardrobes, drawers, laundry containers, etc., and carefully place in piles on the bed or a convenient clear space
9. Remove hangers from items, disposing of any which are surplus, broken or unsuitable
10. Remove any non-fixed storage solutions from wardrobes and drawers
11. Vacuum, clean, and polish your wardrobe as necessary

Make your own natural air freshener

1. Get a spray bottle with a fine nozzle
2. Add a cup of water
3. Mix in about 10 drops of room-purifying* essential oil
4. Gently spray around the room

*lemon/pine/eucalyptus/grapefruit/lavender

Tips for getting the most out of your session

- Do your hair and make-up as usual so you feel at your best
- Wear something like a dressing gown that you can easily put on and take off
- Put on good underwear so you'll look streamlined in every outfit
- Have a pair of tights readily available to try with skirts and dresses if required

part 7

wardrobe worthiness test

Declutter Therapy™

wardrobe worthiness Test

Ask yourself these four simple questions for every single item of clothing, footwear, accessory, and jewellery you own to ensure it's worthy of your wardrobe. Immediately place the item in the correct pile as you make your decision.

The wardrobe worthiness Test

1. Do you love it?
    - It makes you feel stylish, happy, and confident
    - It reflects your individual style
    - You've worn it in the last 18 months
2. Does it physically suit you?
    - It fits perfectly and it is comfortable
    - It flatters your colouring (hair colour, eye colour, skin tone)
    - It works for your height, size, and body shape
3. Does it work for your personal requirements?
    - It is age-appropriate
    - It is relevant to your lifestyle
    - It is suitable for your climate
4. Is it in good condition?
    - It is in its original colour and shape
    - It is tear-free/stain-free/damage-free
    - It is clean and fresh

Some Decluttering Exceptions

- Items that don't fit perfectly and are worth altering
- Special-occasion dresses, shoes or accessories that you haven't had reasonable opportunity to wear in over 18 months
- Items you haven't worn in over 18 months that you've been sparing
- Timeless jackets and coats like blazers and trenches
- Antique or vintage handbags or jewellery
- Suits for infrequent formal occasions such as interviews
- Wedding dress/shoes/veil
- Items that fail some or all of the Wardrobe Worthiness Test but that you genuinely need for the moment

Of course, if you come across something that fails one or more of the Wardrobe Worthiness Test questions and you still want to keep it, do. Just be honest with yourself. If you don't look forward to wearing it and you know you'll always wear something else first, it needs to go! Remember that getting rid of a sentimental item won't destroy a positive memory. For such items that you can't justify keeping consider taking a photo or a fabric swatch before you discard. If you love the fabric but hate the cut, think about making the item into something else.

Orchid

Tips for making the right decision

- Consult your full-length mirror
- Try everything on
- Focus on fit over size on the tag
- Avoid rehandling items

Part 8

Tidy up

DeclutterTherapy™

Tidy up

Now that you've completed the Wardrobe Worthiness Test, it's time to tidy up your living space. Some actions you'll need to undertake straight away so you can resume normal function. Other actions - although vital to the success of the process - can be left until you've more time and energy.

Actions to carry out immediately

- ☐ Repaint/replace wardrobe doors
- ☐ Place items from the laundry pile in your laundry container
- ☐ Put items from the following piles in clearly labelled bags:
    - ☐ dry cleaner
    - ☐ dressmaker/cobbler
    - ☐ give/sell/exchange/donate/recycle
- ☐ Dispose of items for the bin
- ☐ Return any non-fixed storage solutions to their place as required
- ☐ Return items you are keeping to your wardrobe, drawers, etc. and organise

Don't panic if you've returned very little to the wardrobe – you're keeping only items you love, want, and need. As long as you've enough to keep you feeling confident and environment-appropriate for the coming while, there's no need to worry.

Actions to carry out as soon as possible

- ☐ Complete the Wardrobe Stock-take
- ☐ Send items to the dry cleaner, dressmaker or cobbler as required
- ☐ Give, sell, exchange, donate or recycle unwanted items as originally intended
- ☐ Dispose of any old unwanted storage solutions as appropriate
- ☐ Buy storage solutions you need and integrate as necessary

Part 9

wardrobe stock-take

Declutter Therapy™

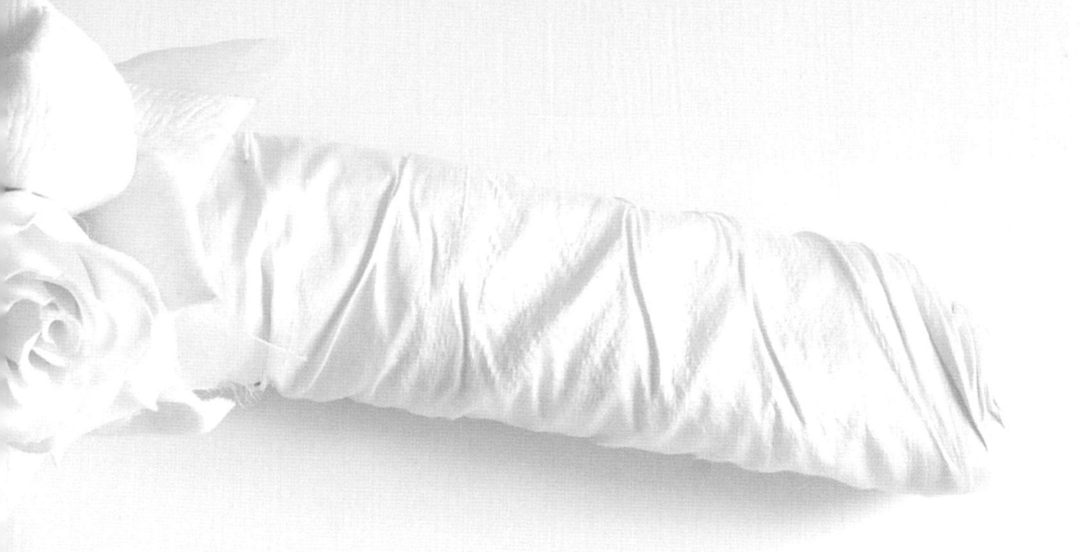

wardrobe stock-take

As you have now assessed the Wardrobe Worthiness of everything you own, let's take stock of what you've put back into your wardrobe. This activity will give you a good sense of where you are style-wise and will allow you to identify gaps in your wardrobe. Keep your lifestyle activities in mind so you can focus on what you might need.

CLOTHING	NO. OF ITEMS	WHAT I NEED
skirts		
trousers		
jeans		
suits		
jackets		
coats		
jumpers/cardigans		
tops		
blouses/shirts		
tracksuits		
swimwear		
other		
other		

FOOTWEAR	NO. OF ITEMS	WHAT I NEED
shoes		
boots		
sandals		
flip-flops		
other		
other		

UNDERWEAR	NO. OF ITEMS	WHAT I NEED
Bras		
Panties		
Tights/stockings		
Socks		
Nightwear		
Other		
Other		

ACCESSORIES	NO. OF ITEMS	WHAT I NEED
Handbags/purses		
Belts		
Scarves		
Hats/caps		
Gloves		
Other		
Other		

JEWELLERY	NO. OF ITEMS	WHAT I NEED
Necklaces		
Earrings		
Bracelets		
Rings		
Watches		
Brooches		
Other		
Other		

Part 10

Wardrobe Maintenance

Declutter Therapy™

wardrobe maintenance

Congratulations on your tidy, systematic, and relevant wardrobe - now all you have to do is maintain it! By carrying out a little regular upkeep you'll never need a decluttering session of such magnitude again.

Wardrobe maintenance includes the everyday chores of cleaning, tidying, and organising, as well as decluttering. To aid continual decluttering, simply designate a good-sized box, basket or bag to an accessible place, ideally the bottom of your wardrobe. Any time you flick through the wardrobe and find an item you no longer need or love, simply add it to the container. The convenience and visibility of the container encourages you to sacrifice items as soon as you're ready to part with them. If possible, avoid see-through containers in case you're attracted back to something you would have otherwise happily forgotten about. Distribute the contents of this container regularly to eliminate temptation and help keep your wardrobe in a healthy state.

Consistently maintaining your decluttered wardrobe allows further refinement of your personal style as well as ensuring the contents are age and lifestyle appropriate. Your climate will dictate the frequency and time of your seasonal decluttering efforts. Following the 'one-in, one-out' policy as you shop also helps to keep your wardrobe streamlined and up-to-date.

Carry out the following activities routinely to maintain your decluttered wardrobe.

Daily

- ☐ Put dirty clothes in laundry container
- ☐ Hang up clean clothes or place on shelves or in drawers
- ☐ Return footwear, accessories, and jewellery to their place

Weekly

- ☐ Sort and wash laundry
- ☐ Iron clothing
- ☐ Polish footwear
- ☐ Send clothes to dry cleaner

Monthly

- ☐ Tidy and regroup items as desired
- ☐ Send items for alteration or repair
- ☐ Add contents of decluttering container and other unwanted items to bags and distribute

Seasonally

- ☐ Swap in and swap out items as per season
- ☐ Clean inside of wardrobe
- ☐ Reorganise items to best advantage
- ☐ Add contents of decluttering container and other unwanted items to bags and distribute

Any spare time you have can benefit your wardrobe. It can take just five minutes to declutter a sock drawer, ten minutes to rearrange your jewellery, and twenty minutes to refold your shelved clothing.

If you feel like you may have difficulty maintaining your newly decluttered wardrobe, consider setting simple, achievable goals to help keep you focused and motivated. For example, 'Every night just before I go to bed I'll spend five minutes sorting out, organising, and storing away the clothes, footwear, accessories, and jewellery I've worn or tried on that day.'

My Declutter Therapy™ Goals

conclusion

Declutter Therapy™

conclusion

Throughout Declutter Therapy™ the ultimate wardrobe decluttering experience, you have enjoyed the therapeutic benefits of the wardrobe decluttering process. You have gained access to the mindset, knowledge, and tools to help create positive change in your life.

The Declutter Therapy™ Process Overview

- Declutter Therapy™ Mindset and Benefits
- Toolkit and Preparation
- Wardrobe Worthiness Test
- Tidy Up
  - Organise
  - Distribute Unwanted Items
  - Storage
- Wardrobe Stock-take
  - Selective Shopping
- Wardrobe Maintenance

Declutter Therapy™ is your life-long guide to decluttering and shopping. Cherish it – it is a valuable reminder of what you have experienced and how far you have come.

Further Information

If you've any questions or comments on Declutter Therapy™ please contact *declutertherapy@lifestylecoach.ie*

To learn more about the author Breda Stack and her company LifeStyle Coach you can visit *www.lifestylecoach.ie*

Sign up for monthly TOP TIPS on style, decluttering and lifestyle at *TOPTIPS@lifestylecoach.ie*